It's 5 o'clock Somewhere

THE GLOBAL GUIDE TO
FABULOUS COCKTAILS

Colleen Mullaney

It's 5 o'clock Somewhere

THE GLOBAL GUIDE TO
FABULOUS COCKTAILS

Colleen Mullaney

sixth&spring books

233 Spring Street
New York, NY 10013

sixth&spring books

233 Spring Street
New York, NY 10013

Editorial Director
ELAINE SILVERSTEIN

Book Division Manager
WENDY WILLIAMS

Senior Editor
MICHELLE BREDESON

Copy Editor
KRISTINA SIGLER

Art Director
DIANE LAMPHRON

Book Design
JANEEN BELLAFIORE

Associate Art Director
SHEENA T. PAUL

Photography
JACK DEUTSCH

Bookings Manager
RACHAEL STEIN

———

Vice President, Publisher
TRISHA MALCOLM

Production Manager
DAVID JOINNIDES

Creative Director
JOE VIOR

President
ART JOINNIDES

Library of Congress Control Number: 2008925034

ISBN 10: 1-933027-62-2
ISBN 13: 978-1-933027-62-3

Manufactured in China

1 3 5 7 9 10 8 6 4 2

First Edition

Acknowledgments

I would like to raise a glass to all who had a special part in this global journey:

* A special toast to Joe Dance of Crate and Barrel for loaning all the beautiful barware and tools.

* To Jack Deutsch, my photographer and friend, who always works to find the magic in every shot, and can always be counted on to taste the props.

* To Laura, my stylist *de rigueur* and master of ice cubes— thanks for another wonderful result.

* To my publisher, Sixth&Spring Books, especially Trisha and Art, who finally decided that perhaps a cocktail or two isn't such a bad thing.

* To my brothers Bill, Kevin and Michael, because they said I had to credit them once for something, so it might as well be cocktails; and to my parents, especially my mom, because there are so many places we have yet to go where it's 5 o'clock.

I LOVE YOU ALL. CHEERS!

This book is dedicated to my husband, Jack, who always knows when it's 5 o'clock somewhere.

Contents

It all started for me at 5 o'clock...

...on a trip to Paris a few years ago. I was sipping a champagne cocktail in a fabulous hotel lobby bar, listening to music and munching on those delectable bar snacks. I suddenly thought, This is what we all need—to visit all the luxe and fabulous places around the globe and sample what they serve for their 5 o'clock cocktail. But then I thought, Who but the jet set could manage this world tour of mixology?

At that moment, my quest turned into a more important one: Could I re-create this global cocktail experience and make it one that everyone could enjoy? It would have to include four things: exotic locales around the globe; the consummate local libation; snacks or nibbles; and, of course, the all-important music playlist—because it really isn't a party unless there is music on the hi-fi, or, in this day and age, a docked iPod.

I wanted to write a book that travels for you, and here it is, complete with an playlist of world rhythms. After all, if it's all about entertaining your friends, why not do it with international flair? We'll begin in London, the home of Greenwich Mean Time and the first 5 o'clock bell, tolled by none other than the world's most famous clock, Big Ben. So sit back, flip through the pages and download the playlist on the opposite page—there are more suggestions listed with the cocktails themselves, but the inspiration was larger than the space we could give it here.

Now go get inspired and get mixing!

Colleen

SONG	ARTIST	ALBUM
1. Russia Privjet	Basshunter	LOL
2. Cordoba	Vicente Amigo	Ciudad de Las Ideas
3. Casino Royale	Herb Alpert & The Tijuana Brass	Sounds Like
4. Consolação	Celso Fonseca	Natural
5. Night Over Manaus (Original Mix)	Boozoo Bajou	Get Your Stereo Deluxed
6. Bamboleo	Gypsy Rebels	Gypsy Kings & Queens
7. Camel's Rhythm	Upper Egypt Ensemble	Egypt—A Musical Voyage
8. Katharin aus Krotoschin	Kathe Erlholz (From "Die Lichter von Berlin")	Cabaret Berlin Vol. 1
9. Amor Verdadero	Afro Cuban All Stars	A Toda Cuba Le Gusta
10. Come On, Let's Go	Los Lobos	Los Lobos: Just Another Band from East L.A
11. Wicked Game	Chris Isaak	Best of Chris Isaak (Remastered)
12. Faster Than Cars Drive	Kate Tucker & the Sons of Sweden	Kate Tucker & the Sons of Sweden
13. Sway	Michael Bublé	Michael Bublé
14. Push	Enrique Iglesias	Insomniac
15. Desert Rose	Sting	Brand New Day
16. The Girl from Ipanema	Astrud Gilberto	Cocktail Disco (Bonus Track Version)
17. Coconut Woman	Harry Belafonte	Harry Belafonte: Greatest Hits
18. Summertime	Kenny Chesney	The Road and the Radio

It's 5 o'clock Somewhere

DOWNLOAD THIS LIST
FROM iTUNES

Europe

The journey around the globe kicks off here, so let the mixing and magic start where cocktails became couture.

London, England

PASSIONFRUIT MARTINI

SERVES 4

- 8 oz./237ml Absolut Mandrin vodka
- 8 oz./237ml passionfruit nectar
- 8 oz./237ml pineapple juice

Pineapple chunks for garnish

Pour all ingredients into a shaker filled with ice and mix well. Strain into glasses. Garnish each with a pineapple chunk and serve.

SERVE WITH:
Huntsman cheese and water crackers

Always hip and happening, London is an ever-trendy destination for all the latest in fashion, music and gastronomy. This special libation is from the Light Bar in the sleek and stylish St. Martin's Lane Hotel, a boutique hotel designed by Philippe Starck and located in the hub of the West End. On your way back from shopping at Harvey Nichols, stop in for the Light's stirring Passionfruit Martini. (You'll find our version slightly lighter on the fruit and heavier on the passion.)

london

ON THE HI-FI
Coldplay

13

London, England

GREEN VELVET MARTINI

SERVES 4

- 8 oz./237ml Gordon's gin
- 2 oz./59ml apricot brandy
- 2 oz./59ml Noilly Prat
- 2 oz./59ml green crème de menthe

Cherries or apple slices for garnish

Pour all ingredients into a shaker with ice and mix well. Strain into martini glasses, garnish with an apple wedge or cherry, and serve.

SERVE WITH:
Cheese crackers

There are so many trendy bars and terrific cocktails in this great city, we had to give merry ole' England another page in the book. After shopping at world-famous Harrods or attending floral classes at Paula Pryke's Flower School, I head to the Lobby Bar at One Aldwych in Covent Garden, where they serve up a rainbow of cocktails, including the Green Velvet Martini. Although they make it with a cherry on the other side of the Atlantic, if you prefer, a small slice of apple will do quite well.

ON THE HI-FI
Pet Shop Boys, *Discography*

london

Edinburgh, Scotland

THE TARTAN

12 oz./355ml Drambuie
12 oz./355ml club soda
 6 oz./177ml sour mix
 6 oz./177ml cola
Lemon wedges for garnish

In a large shaker, mix
Drambuie and sour mix. Fill
glasses with ice and divide
mixture equally. Pour cola
and club soda into each
glass to fill. Squeeze one
lemon wedge into each
cocktail. Serve immediately.

SERVE WITH:
Fig, bacon and blue cheese
quesadillas

Taking up the hilly northern third of the isle of Great Britain and surrounded by water on three sides, Scotland is big on outdoor life. You can trek in the Highlands, swim in the sea or putt a few on the links at St. Andrews. After so much fresh air, you might be inclined to take in downtown Edinburgh, where the Bollinger Bar at Palm Court (in the Balmoral Hotel) can easily refresh and replenish you. The bar serves up some fine cocktails—the Tartan in particular is quite a drink. The Drambuie, with its unique herbal and honeyed flavors, makes for a great drink any time of the year.

edinburgh

ON THE HI-FI
The soundtrack from
Four Weddings and a Funeral

Dublin, Ireland

SHINZER

SERVES 4

12 oz./355ml ruby-red
   grapefruit juice
 8 oz./237ml vodka
 4 oz./118ml limoncello

Pour juice, limoncello and
vodka into a shaker filled
with ice and mix well.
Pour into chilled cocktail
glasses.

SERVE WITH:
Mild cheddar cheese and
crackers or bread

If there's one place in Europe that's
experienced a major boom in terms of
art, culture and attitude, it's the city on
the River Liffey. Dublin profited well
from the boom times of the 1990s and
continues to attract new jobs, new
energy and an intensely hip social
scene—no wonder it's a popular destination for the young, cool European set.
This cocktail is named after my friend
Sinead (Shinzer is her nickname),
because it's her favorite libation. The
citrus zing of the grapefruit blends
perfectly with the vodka and lemon.
Although I've sampled many a cocktail
throughout Dublin, this one is a real
standout. Be sure to make a big batch
if friends are stopping by!

dublin

ON THE HI-FI
U2 or The Coors

Berlin, Germany

IMPERIAL

SERVES 4

8 oz./177ml dry
vermouth
6 oz./177ml gin
2 oz./59ml maraschino
liqueur
1 dash bitters
Cherries or lemon peels
for garnish

Pour all ingredients into a
cocktail shaker filled with
ice and mix well. Strain
into cocktail glasses.
Garnish with a cherry or
lemon peel and serve.

SERVE WITH:
Soft pretzel sticks

In the almost two decades since its
wall came tumbling down, Berlin has
been a hot spot on the rise. Germany's
largest city is home to great avant-
garde artists, designers and cultural
impresarios. It has the largest train
station in Europe, and it recently
hosted the World Cup to boot. The
reigning cocktails are on the non-fussy
side; the Imperial is one of the best.

ON THE HI-FI
Rudolph Nelson, *Cabaret Berlin,
Vol. 1*

Barcelona, Spain

STRAWBERRY POM MOJITO

SERVES 4

- 8 mint leaves
- 8 lime slices
- 8 strawberries, diced
- 4 tsp./20g sugar or
- 2 oz./59ml simple syrup (see recipe on page 144)
- 8 oz./237ml Bacardi Superior rum
- 2 oz./59ml pomegranate juice
- 2 oz./59ml lime juice

Seltzer or club soda
Extra mint leaves and strawberries for garnish

Combine mint, lime slices, diced strawberry and sugar in a cocktail shaker. Muddle together and add, rum, pomegranate juice and lime juice. Pour into ice-filled glasses. Top with seltzer. Garnish with a strawberry and mint leaf.

SERVE WITH:
Manchego cheese "points" topped with tapenade

After a day spent pounding the pavement, taking in the Catalan capital's amazing modernist architecture—all that Art Nouveau and Gaudí—this cocktail will put some pep back in your step, just in time for Barcelona's sophisticated nightlife. The sweetness of the strawberries hits precisely the right note to balance the tang of fresh lime and pomegranate juices. The recipe here adds a little twist to the most popular cocktail of the moment, making this mojito even tastier.

ON THE HI-FI
Estrella Morente and Vicente Amigo

barcelona

Capri, Italy

LEMON GROTTO

SERVES 4

- 6 oz./177ml limoncello
- 2 oz./59ml Grand Marnier
- 24 oz./710ml champagne
- 8 medium-sized strawberries

Fresh mint sprigs for garnish

Slice and soak the strawberries in limoncello and Grand Marnier for at least 1 hour. Purée this mixture in a blender or food processor and pour evenly into champagne flutes. Add champagne to fill each flute. Garnish with a sprig of mint and serve immediately.

SERVE WITH:
A variety of olives, warmed potato chips and mixed nuts

Lying just off of the Amalfi coast, the island of Capri is a 30-minute ferry ride from the fishing village of Positano. Although Capri appears at first to be a giant rock set in the turquoise Mediterranean, at closer glance, one can see fashionable homes, hotels and designer boutiques. While strolling about Capri enjoying the scent of bougainvillea, look for the yellow and white awnings of the famed Grand Hotel Quisisana (meaning "here one heals"), where Europe's rich and famous imbibe into the wee hours. As the recipe of the hotel's Champagne Cocktail is kept under lock and key, the version here was created after sampling many originals.

capri

ON THE HI-FI
Celso Fonseca, *Natural*

Fiesole, Italy

KIR IMPERIAL

SERVES 4

- 4 oz./118ml Cointreau
- 4 oz./118ml crème de framboise
- 1 bottle (750ml) Brut champagne

Orange peel for garnish

Pour a dash of Cointreau and crème de framboise into each flute. Top with chilled champagne and garnish with an orange peel. Serve immediately.

SERVE WITH:

Cheese sticks

High in the hills above Florence in the village of Fiesole lies the Villa San Michele, a former Franciscan monastery. This classy hotel boasts the most spectacular views of nearby Florence at sunset—you can see the Duomo sparkling in the fading light. And nothing beats sitting on the veranda enjoying a cocktail before dinner—in this region, the art of living is as magnificent as the art of Michelangelo. This drink, the Kir Imperial, was invented here at the Villa San Michele by a barman in the 1940s and is still on the menu today. They use rosé champagne, but a nice Brut works well, too.

ON THE HI-FI
Andrea Bocelli

Rome, Italy

THE CONFESSION

SERVES 4

- 4 oz./118ml grappa
- 4 oz./118ml cherry liqueur
- 1 bottle (750ml) champagne

Pour ingredients evenly into flute glasses. Top off with champagne and serve.

SERVE WITH:
Prosciutto-wrapped melon slices

Oh, to have cocktails in the "Eternal City," such a vibrant and romantic destination. Here you'll find many modern boutique hotels housed in what used to be banks or government buildings—and all are surrounded by new places to meet for cocktails. Walk into the Zest Bar and stand (nobody, it seems, ever sits in Rome) among the fashionistas, sipping a Confession. Have one or two while thinking of gamine Audrey Hepburn in the classic film *Roman Holiday*.

rome

ON THE HI-FI
Il Divo

Lake Como, Italy

LAKE COMO

SERVES 4

- 8 oz./237ml vodka
- 4 oz./118ml red currant juice
- 4 oz./118ml cranberry juice

Splash of fresh lime juice

- 2 tsp./10g brown sugar

Fresh lime wedges for garnish

Mix all ingredients in cocktail shaker. Pour into ice-filled glasses. Garnish with lime wedges.

SERVE WITH:
Cheese puffs

Ahh, the beauty of it all.... The pristine blue-green of Lake Como set against snow-capped mountains makes for a glorious view. Nestled along the lake is the tony town of Bellagio, where you'll find the Mezzaluna Bar and its fine cocktail offerings. The specialty of the house is the Lake Como. The delightful contrast between the sweetness of the juices and the bite of the vodka make for a lovely brew.

lake como

ON THE HI-FI
Awake by Josh Groban

Ibiza, Spain

SANGRIA
SERVES 8

- 1 bottle (750ml) rosé wine
- 8 oz./237ml Spanish brandy
- 4 oz./118ml Cointreau
- 4 oz./118ml orange juice
- 8 oz./237ml sparkling water
- 2 oz./59ml fresh lime juice
- 4 cups of ice cubes

Lemon, lime and orange slices for garnish

Combine wine, brandy, Cointreau, orange and lime juices and fruit slices in a large pitcher and mix well. Chill for at least 30 minutes to allow flavors to marry. Just before serving, slowly pour in the sparkling water and add ice cubes.

SERVE WITH:
Grilled garlic shrimp on skewers

Although this island is tiny, don't let that fool you—more partying energy is expended here per square foot than anywhere else on earth. Lying off the east coast of Spain, stylish Ibiza has superb beaches with many hidden coves to explore. After a quick swim in crystal-clear waters, why not lounge on your chaise and sip some fruity sangria? This way you can at least pack a few vitamins in before you head out to drink all night at villa bashes and yacht happenings. This recipe is based on the Balearic Island classic.

ON THE HI-FI
Sade, *Love Deluxe*

ibiza

Paris, France

BACCARAT
SERVES 4

- 6 oz./177ml cranberry juice
- 2 oz./59ml lime juice
- 8 oz./237ml Grand Marnier
- 16 oz./473ml rosé champagne

In a cocktail shaker, mix cranberry juice, lime juice and Grand Marnier. Divide equally among champagne flutes. Top with champagne and serve.

SERVE WITH:
Toasted baguette slices with tapenade

In the City of Light, where champagne goes hand in hand with moonlit walks along the river Seine, there is so much to do and see, it can be nearly overwhelming. You can *reste calme* with a Baccarat, the most delicious cocktail this side of the Eiffel Tower. You might want to sample one at the magnificent Hotel Crillon, a stone's throw from the Champs-Elysées. The Crillon and its famed Piano Bar resonate with luxury and are the perfect place to sip the house specialty. The light, sweet fruit juices lend a freshness to the dry champagne; be sure to have enough bubbly on hand for refills.

paris

ON THE HI-FI
Stéphane Pompougnac,
Hotel Costes: Vol. 9

Stockholm, Sweden

WILD STRAWBERRY SOUR

SERVES 4

8 oz./237ml Svensk
    vodka
2 oz./59ml Chambord
2 oz./59ml fresh lemon
    juice
2 oz./59ml simple syrup
    (see recipe on page 144)
12 fresh strawberries
Fresh mint for garnish

In a cocktail shaker or
large glass, muddle together
the vodka, Chambord,
lemon juice, syrup and 8
strawberries. Strain into
glasses filled with crushed
ice. Garnish each glass with
a strawberry and sprig of
mint.

SERVE WITH:
Salmon-and-cream-cheese
dip with crackers

This design-mad city, surrounded by a gorgeous 24,000-island archipelago, is home to more single people than any other European capital—no wonder it has energy to rival a power plant and plenty of topnotch bars and restaurants for entertaining. Vodka is a main ingredient in many Swedish cocktails, and for my version of the strawberry sour, I've added Chambord liqueur for a delightfully smooth finish. The name is a tribute to the Ingmar Bergman film *Wild Strawberries*.

stockholm

ON THE HI-FI
Abba, *Abba Gold*

37

Vienna, Austria

THE EMPEROR

SERVES 4

- 8 oz./237ml espresso
- 4 oz./118ml Absolut Vanilia vodka
- 4 oz./118ml Kahlúa
- 4 oz./118ml light cream or milk
- 8 oz./237ml heavy cream for whipping

Coffee beans for garnish

Prepare espresso. Warm light cream or milk. Pour espresso evenly into 4 glasses and top with milk. Add vodka and Kahlúa. Whip heavy cream until soft peaks form. Top off each serving with a heaping spoonful of whipped cream. Garnish with coffee beans.

SERVE WITH:
Simple shortbread cookies

It's not all Wiener schnitzel here: this vibrant city is in the midst of a culinary revolution. You'll find an intermingling of Mediterranean influences, Kaffeehäuser (cafes) with good wine lists, and vineyards right outside the city limits. The art scene is also extremely enticing—why not check out the world-famous Vienna Boys' Choir? The Emperor makes a divine after-dinner treat. If you can't use espresso, strong coffee will do the trick. This recipe is fashioned after the coffee cocktail they serve at Café Mozart in the Style Hotel.

ON THE HI-FI
Classical music, of course

vienna

Budva, Montenegro

MONTENEGRO CRUSH

SERVES 4

  8 oz./237ml herb-infused
    gin
  3 sprigs fresh mint
Cucumber slices for
garnish

In a large shaker, muddle
sprigs of mint with gin.
Add ice and shake until
frothy. Strain into glasses
and serve immediately.
Garnish with cucumber
slices.

SERVE WITH:
Mixed nuts

This modern-day Casbah, with its
magnificent old-world charm and
fine-estates-cum-luxury-hotels dotting
the jagged coastline, makes for a
dramatic setting. This is a hot spot
for young swingers, a relatively new
playground where the nights are
arguably more important than the
days. The cocktail of the moment is
the Crush, a smooth and enticing
drink with a cool, crisp finish. It suits
equally a casual gathering of friends
or a swanky dinner party.

budva

ON THE HI-FI
The soundtrack from
Casino Royale

Santorini, Greece

PASSIONFRUIT MOJITO

SERVES 4

20 oz./591ml light rum
 2 oz./118ml mint-infused simple syrup (see recipe on page 144)
 8 oz./237ml passionfruit nectar
 1 lime, cut in slices, plus more for garnish
12 fresh mint leaves
 4 cups crushed ice
Club soda

Muddle the mint, lime slices, simple syrup, passionfruit nectar and rum in a large glass or cocktail shaker. Divide mixture evenly into glasses. Fill glasses with crushed ice, top with soda and mix well. Garnish with twist of lime. Serve immediately.

SERVE WITH:
Feta-stuffed grape leaves

Azure waters give way to caves and charming villages perched on a dramatically rocky landscape. If you can survive the donkey ride up from the marina here, you'll definitely want liquid refreshment. This recipe builds on the most popular drink on the international social scene, the mojito. The passionfruit turns the mojito a calming pastel hue, which should put you in mind of the tranquil, white-washed buildings and blue sea beyond Santorini's Athena bar.

ON THE HI-FI
Kraounakis/Papayiannopoulou, "Malamo"

santorini

Moscow, Russia

RED SKY

SERVES 4

- 8 oz./237ml vodka, chilled
- 4 oz./118ml Chambord
- 4 oz./118ml pomegranate juice
- 2 oz./59ml fresh lime juice

Splash of club soda

Twists of lime for garnish

Mix all ingredients except soda in a shaker filled with ice. Strain into glasses. Top with a splash of soda, garnish with a lime twist and serve.

SERVE WITH:
Salmon and caviar pie

The pairing of new wealth and youth in Moscow has revitalized the city, making it a dynamic, intriguing place that juxtaposes old with new. Against a backdrop of historic churches and monuments, Moscow's young professionals are enjoying it all. The cocktail of the moment involves vodka (of course), with a few juices thrown in for good measure (and to temper the alcohol). Our version of the Red Sky has been "lightened" a bit with club soda. If you're feeling daring, go light on the lightening.

moscow

ON THE HI-FI
Basshunter, *LOL*

Africa

From bustling cities to desert plains to oceans blue, rhythms rise and fall, and cocktails reign supreme.

Casablanca, Morocco

casablanca

OASIS
SERVES 4

8 oz./237ml gin
4 oz./118ml papaya
  nectar
2 oz./59ml lemon juice
Club soda
Orange, lemon and lime
slices for garnish

In an ice-filled shaker, mix
the first three ingredients
together and then shake
well. Strain the mixture
into ice-filled glasses and
top with club soda.
Garnish with orange,
lemon and lime slices and
serve.

SERVE WITH:
An array of olives and
rosemary crostini

The largest city in Morocco is best
known for the oft-quoted cinematic
line "Here's looking at you, kid"—
uttered by the handsomely raffish
Humphrey Bogart to screen siren
Ingrid Bergman in the 1942 film that
shares its name. In 2004, Rick's Café
(based on the set design in the movie)
opened in the Old Medina section of
the city. It's a restaurant and bonafide
piano bar where pianist Issam plays a
mean rendition of the classic "As Time
Goes By." You, too, can re-create the
movie by mixing up a batch of Oasis—
the most fitting cocktail for a friendly
gathering of cinephiles.

ON THE HI-FI
Faraò/Durham/Zunio,
"Fascinating"

48

Lagos, Nigeria

BLACKBERRY BRAMBLE

SERVES 4

- 8 oz./237ml gin
- 4 oz./118ml crème de cassis
- 2 oz./59ml lemon juice
- 2 oz./59ml simple syrup (see recipe on page 144)

Club soda

Blackberries for garnish

Blend all ingredients in a shaker or pitcher. Pour mixture into ice-filled glasses. Top off each glass with club soda and garnish with fresh blackberries.

SERVE WITH:
Plantain chips and fruit-based salsa

Though the West African country of Nigeria is bordered by Chad, Cameroon, Niger and the Republic of Benin, it's not landlocked. Lagos, Nigeria's largest city, located on islands around a lagoon and the Atlantic, has modern hotels and cocktail lounges to host the growing number of travelers who descend here. The Bramble, with its blackberry tang, is a cocktail favored here for its fruity kick and refreshing taste. If blackberry doesn't float your boat, swap out the crème de cassis for raspberry, strawberry, orange, apricot or peach liqueur—they're all tasty choices.

ON THE HI-FI
Fela Kuti and King Sunny Adé

Cape Town, South Africa

STARDUST

SERVES 4

- 8 oz./237ml Absolut Citron vodka
- 8 oz./237ml peach schnapps
- 4 oz./118ml blue Curaçao
- 2 oz./59ml sour mix
- 2 oz./59ml pineapple juice

Star (carambola) fruit or kiwi for garnish.

Mix all the ingredients in a large shaker filled with ice. Blend until frothy and cold. Strain into cocktail glasses, garnish with kiwi stars and serve.

TRICKS OF THE TRADE:

To form stars from kiwi, cut fruit into ¼-inch slices and, face down on a cutting board, cut away perimeter or ends of fruit to create points of a star.

SERVE WITH:

Thick-cut potato chips or salted soy nuts

You'll find an interesting array of cocktails in this third-largest city in South Africa. You may want to start off visiting some of the trendy places to down a drink, like the Planet Champagne Bar in the chic Mount Nelson Hotel. Sit yourself down on those sleek white patent-leather sofas and order a Stardust from Benson, the head barman. Though it's not a champagne drink, this delicious, perfectly balanced cocktail is a real tour de force.

ON THE HI-FI
Youssou N'Dour, *Rokku Mi Rokka*

Port Louis, Mauritius

SANGRIA BONITA
SERVES 6

1 bottle dry white wine
4 oz./118ml Cointreau
½ 750ml-bottle Perrier
3 tbsp./43g sugar
Slices of orange, star fruit,
lime and strawberries
Fresh mint leaves for
garnish

Pour wine, Cointreau and
sparkling water into a large
pitcher. Slowly add sugar
and stir until dissolved.
Add fruit to pitcher and
chill mixture for up to an
hour, allowing the flavors
to marry. Garnish with
mint and serve.

SERVE WITH:
Prosciutto-wrapped
asparagus spears

In describing this once volcanic, now
sumptuously beachy island, surrounded
by coral reefs in the warm Indian
Ocean, one would not be remiss in
using the word "paradise." Just suck on
a freshly cut stalk of the isle's legendary
sugarcane for a taste of that paradise.
You'll find the who's who discreetly
tucked away here, sipping Sangria
Bonita while softly swinging in a
hammock. This recipe is a lighter version
of the typical red-wine sangria—just
the ticket for an after-scuba thirst
quencher or a languorous Sunday
brunch.

port louis

ON THE HI-FI
DJ Alex J, *Downtown Café*

Cairo, Egypt

KING'S RANSOM

SERVES 4

- 8 oz./237ml whiskey
- 4 oz./118ml sweet vermouth
- 2 drops bitters

Splash of lemon juice
Lemon peels for garnish

Mix all ingredients in shaker with ice. Strain into chilled glasses. Garnish with lemon twists.

TRICKS OF THE TRADE:
To make a citrus curl: Use a sharp knife to pare off a thin piece of the outer skin. Remove any white pith, as it has a bitter taste. For a longer, thinner twist, use a zester. To curl twist, wrap it tightly around the handle of a spoon or other long-handled bar tool.

SERVE WITH:
Lobster wontons

Cairo is a wondrously diverse, crowded, noisy and chaotic city where ancient and modern are often seen literally side-by-side—the Great Pyramids of Giza are right on the edge of the city. Whiskey is the drink of choice here for those who indulge in spirits. From the young cocktail crowd to the old guard, this libation rules the town. The King's Ransom is a potent cocktail, so if you're looking for something a bit smoother, try mixing fresh lemonade and a sprig of mint in place of the vermouth and bitters.

ON THE HI-FI
Upper Egypt Ensemble,
Egypt: A Musical Voyage

cairo

Zanzibar, Tanzania

SEX ON THE BEACH

SERVES 4

8 oz./237ml vodka
8 oz./237ml peach
  schnapps
8 oz./237ml cranberry
  juice
4 oz./118ml orange juice
Slices of orange and lime

In a pitcher or cocktail
shaker, mix together the
first four ingredients. Pour
into ice-filled glasses.
Garnish with slices of
orange and lime and serve.

SERVE WITH:
Spicy shrimp on skewers

Sporting glorious wide beaches and bazaars packed with goods from international destinations, the archipelago of Zanzibar lies in the Indian Ocean just off the coast of its nation, Tanzania. *Karibu* means welcome in Swahili, the official language, and serving your guests the mouthwatering and sensually named "SOB" is certainly one way to provide a warm welcome! Have numerous pitchers of this cocktail on hand, and you're sure to get your party started.

ON THE HI-FI
Sting, "Desert Rose"

Mombasa, Kenya

RASPBERRY DAWA

SERVES 4

12 oz./355ml lemon vodka
 2 oz./59ml simple syrup
(see recipe on page 144)
Juice of 2 limes
10 raspberries, plus 12
    more for garnish
Lime wedges for garnish
 4 dawa sticks, or
 1 tsp./2g honey

Muddle 10 raspberries in
the bottom of a cocktail
shaker. Mix all other
ingredients together and
strain into ice-filled glasses.
Garnish each glass with 3
raspberries and a lime
wedge. Serve with a dawa
stick or a drizzle ½
teaspoon honey into each
drink.

SERVE WITH:
Salted peanuts

In Mombasa, a port city and gateway
to some of Africa's best eastern
beaches, life seems to pause. Wander
through intriguing marketplaces and
admire the many crafted goods and
the Swahili women in their brightly
printed wraps. Then check out the
Tembo, an outdoor disco that's
thumping 24/7. You'll never forget the
establishment's Lollipop GoGo bar,
where the traditional thirst-quenching
cocktail is mixed with a "dawa" stick—
an African sugar stick. We've substituted
a drizzle of honey here; use a swizzle
stick to do this if you can.

ON THE HI-FI
African ensembles such as
Ladysmith Black Mambazo

Asia

Libations made with native ingredients in fusion with neon lights and a dance-all-night attitude? Just step up to the bar.

Jaipur, India

BLOSSOM

SERVES 4

- 8 oz./237ml Bombay Sapphire gin
- 6 oz./177ml fraises des bois
- 4 oz./118ml martini rosé

Edible rose petals or orchid blossoms for garnish

In a cocktail shaker filled with ice, mix ingredients together. Strain into glasses, garnish with fresh petals and serve.

SERVE WITH:
Ginger cashews

Known as India's "pink city" because of its reddish-pink sandstone buildings, Jaipur is also a sporting haven for aficionados of polo, the game of kings. If you are unable to foot the bill for a horse, you can always resort to the many local elephants. In fact, that's how the game is played on the grounds of the Rambagh Palace, which used to belong to the Maharajah. If you can't afford to play with the kings, you can always drink with them. Head to the Polo Bar and allow head barman Amit Kumar to whip you up a lovely drink. Though he's a martini whiz, his specialty is the Blossom.

jaipur

ON THE HI-FI
Ustad Abdul Halim Jaffer Khan,
Live in Jaipur 1968

Ho Chi Minh City, Vietnam

TYPHOON TINA

SERVES 4

6 oz./177ml gin
4 oz./118ml Cointreau
2 oz./59ml lime juice
Dash of Angostura bitters
Lime peel for garnish

In an ice-filled cocktail shaker, mix together all ingredients. Strain into glasses—each filled with four ice cubes—then garnish and serve.

SERVE WITH:
Sweet-and-sour spareribs and spicy nuts

Ho Chi Minh is complex: a metropolis filled with exquisite beauty, its past tainted by the horrors of war. Now, emerging from its history of unrest, the city is experiencing a renaissance as it looks peacefully toward a brilliant future. In this place of dualities—bicycles gliding alongside high-tech scooters, modern estates crowding up against ancient pagodas—the Typhoon Tina packs a mighty punch, a perfect reflection of the strength of the city's citizens. It's easy to whip up by the batch, and it's a great mood-enhancer to boot.

ho chi minh city

ON THE HI-FI
Pham Duc Thanh, *Vietnamese Traditional Music*

Bangkok, Thailand

BLACK PEARL

SERVES 6

- 6 oz./177ml vodka
- 2 cups/473ml tangerine juice
- 4 oz./118ml lime juice
- 4 oz./118ml crème de cassis
- 1 bottle (750ml) champagne

Lime slices and blackberries for garnish

In a large pitcher, combine juices and vodka. Fill rock glasses with ice cubes. Pour a splash of crème de cassis over the cubes and fill glasses three-quarters full with juice and vodka mixture. Top with champagne. Garnish with lime and berries and serve.

SERVE WITH:
Coconut shrimp and tempura vegetables (order in!)

Though its canals are filled with long-tail boats and its markets bustle morning to night, Bangkok's uniquely laid-back atmosphere beseeches you to find your lotus pad and chill. But not before inviting some friends over to share a batch of Black Pearls. A cocktail that is eminently appropriate for any time of day, this lively concoction's bubbles give it a real kick.

bangkok

ON THE HI-FI
David Fanshawe, *Music from Thailand and Laos*

Shanghai, China

CHAMPAGNE COCKTAIL

SERVES 4

- 4 oz./118ml sake
- 4 oz./118ml ginger vodka

Dash of simple syrup
(see recipe on page 144)

- 1 bottle (750ml) champagne

Lemon peel for garnish

Into each champagne flute, divide and pour even amounts of sake and vodka. Add a dash of simple syrup to each glass and top with champagne. Make lemon peel garnishes by twisting the skin as you peel the lemon (make them long enough to loop several times around the glass, as shown), garnish and serve.

SERVE WITH:
Dim sum, found in gourmet grocery stores or take-out shops

In a city where media moguls, models and stylish foreigners abound, it's not surprising that bars teem with mega-cool mixologists who deftly conjure up delightful concoctions like this Champagne Cocktail. If you're using a sweeter champagne for the cocktail, the simple syrup may not be necessary. *Hint:* Make the lemon peels ahead of time and store them in a bowl with ice and water.

ON THE HI-FI
Liu Fang, *Chinese Traditional Pipa Music*

shanghai

Singapore

SINGAPORE SLING

SERVES 4

- 8 oz./237ml gin
- 4 oz./118ml maraschino liqueur
- 4 oz./118ml Cointreau
- 2 oz./59ml Dom Benedictine
- 2 oz./59ml grenadine
- 1 oz./30ml lime juice
- 8 oz./237ml pineapple juice

Dash of bitters
Pineapple slices for garnish
Cherries for garnish

Pour all ingredients into a large shaker and mix well. Pour into ice-filled glasses, then garnish with pineapple slice and cherry.

SERVE WITH:
Mai fun noodles with coconut shrimp and curry sauce

A city-state known for its rich convergence of cultures, Singapore mixes influences from China, Malaysia, Britain and India. Cultural infusions aside, when it comes to food, noodles are the unanimous favorite. In terms of cocktails, the choice gets a bit more heady—care for the famous Singapore Sling (or the Sing Sling, as it's affectionately known)? This pink lady was invented in the 1910s at the Long Bar in the storied Raffles Hotel. For a consummate party pleaser, mix up a double batch and put the back-up in the fridge to chill.

singapore

ON THE HI-FI
Debu, *Makin Mabuk*

Beijing, China

LYCHEE MARTINI
SERVES 4

8 oz./237ml vodka
12 oz./355ml lychee syrup
2 oz./59ml sugar syrup
Canned lychee fruit for garnish

In a shaker, mix together all ingredients with ice. Strain into glasses, garnish each with a lychee fruit on a cocktail pick and serve.

SERVE WITH:
Crispy chips

This city is more into MTV than Mao, and everyone totes a mobile. Fast-paced Beijing (formerly Peking) is rampantly modernizing, while the rest of China follows not far behind. In the area of the Forbidden City, a number of hip bars offer myriad fabulous cocktails. One of the most popular spots, Suzy Wong's, attracts a glam set that loves to dance until dawn. While lounging on wooden beds (a popular trend in Beijing nightclubs) piled with jewel-toned pillows, these revelers sip the beloved Lychee Martini. Try serving these on poker night, and watch those dice fly!

ON THE HI-FI
Various artists, *Moon Poetry*

Bali, Indonesia

VOODOO

SERVES 4

8 oz./237ml Finlandia
   Mango vodka
8 oz./237ml mango
   nectar
8 lime wedges, plus 4
   more for garnish
12 fresh mint leaves, plus
extra for garnish
Soda

Muddle the mint and the
lime wedges in a cocktail
shaker. Add the mango
nectar and vodka and
allow a few minutes for
the flavors to marry. Put 4
ice cubes in each glass.
Strain mixture into glasses.
Top with soda, garnish
with mint and lime
wedges and serve.

SERVE WITH:
Tapas; oysters on the half-
shell with a fiery sauce

Golden sands and tranquil ocean
breezes fill the day in the otherworldly
aura you find in Bali. Flower-festooned
temples peek out from lush tropical
jungles, and beautiful birdsong fills the
air. Lapping up the serenity are some
new first-class spas—real havens for
travelers. In the stretch between the
jungle and beach lies a bar amid the
sweetly scented palm trees. The
barman serves up a magical cocktail
known as VooDoo. Its bewitching flavor
is sure to keep evil spirits at bay.

ON THE HI-FI
Sabah Habas Mustapha,
Denpasar Moon

77

Hong Kong, China

LEMON GRASS CRUSH

SERVES 4

- 8 oz./237ml vodka
- 2 oz./59ml lemon grass infusion (see recipe on page 144)
- 8 oz./237ml club soda

Splash of lemon juice

Pimiento-stuffed olives for garnish

Into a large cocktail shaker, pour vodka, infusion and lemon juice. Mix well. Pour into ice-filled glasses. Top with club soda. Garnish each with olives on picks and serve.

SERVE WITH:

Deep-fried wontons with sweet-and-sour sauce; chicken skewers with peanut sauce

Once again part of China after over a century of English rule, the diminutive size of this island does nothing to impede its frenetic high energy and wealth of soaring buildings. In this city of international accents, the party lasts all night. A happening place of the moment is the Mandarin Hotel's M Bar. Though the cocktail list is impressive, the favorite libation is by far the tart and sweet Lemon Grass Crush. After all, the subtle intermingling of sweet and sour is a basic in Asian cuisine, so why not enjoy a cocktail of the same ilk?

ON THE HI-FI
DJ Dimi, *Zen Lounge*

Tokyo, Japan

SAKETINI

SERVES 4

8 oz./237ml Absolut
  Mandrin vodka
4 oz./118ml sake
Cucumber slices for
garnish

In a cocktail shaker filled
with ice, mix ingredients.
Strain into glasses.
Garnish with cucumber
slices and serve.

SERVE WITH:

Sushi or fried calamari with
a spicy fruit-based salsa

From its ancient pagodas to its neon-lit tower districts, Tokyo is certainly a delightful combination of Eastern and Western sensibilities. Even better, this Asian fusion has spilled into the realm of cocktails, resulting in some amazingly delicious creations. This sake martini is a unique cross-cultural experience. It makes an elegant and refined before-dinner cocktail of choice, but it's also perfect for a girls'-night-out martini-fest. If you're new to sake, delightfully smooth and rich-tasting Hitorimusume Nigori is the one to taste.

tokyo

ON THE HI-FI
Shoukichi Kina, *Peppermint Tea House*

Australia

Discover the land down under and quench your thirst with some top cocktails.

Melbourne, Australia

LADIES' BLUSH

SERVES 4

- 4 oz./118ml vodka
- 4 oz./118ml raspberry purée
- 2 oz./59ml limoncello
- 1 bottle (750ml) champagne

Raspberries for garnish

In a glass pitcher, mix vodka, raspberry purée and limoncello. Pour evenly into champagne flutes then top with champagne. Garnish with a few raspberries and serve.

SERVE WITH:
Shrimp pizza and lamb croquettes

This sophisticated bayside boomtown has a wide array of food and cocktails to choose from. Though laid back with a groovy undertone, Melbourne has more than its quotient of well-heeled, cosmopolitan fashionistas, and this lovely concoction is the cocktail of the moment. So leave the flip-flops and beer at the beach, whip up a batch of blush and get connected with your inner artist.

melbourne

ON THE HI-FI
Various artists, *Bushfire: Traditional Aboriginal Music*

Sydney, Australia

BONDI CRUSH
SERVES 4

- 4 oz./118ml gin
- 4 oz./118ml Pimm's
- 4 slices ginger
- 4 crushed mint leaves
- 4 oz./118ml watermelon sorbet

In a pitcher, add crushed mint leaves, ginger slices, gin and Pimm's. Stir well, then let sit for 5 minutes to allow flavors to blend. Pour into ice-filled glasses. Top with a small scoop or spoonful of sorbet. Serve immediately.

SERVE WITH:
California sushi rolls; or lemon-tinged hummus with crackers

As the natives know all too well, Sydney is well reputed for its pubs, but has only recently begun to incorporate chic watering holes into the libation mix. But fear not, as this booming capital does now offer some cool places to "bend an elbow," as my Aussie friend would say. Whether that be a bar overlooking popular Bondi Beach or a lush, romantic hot spot on Sydney Harbor's historical Finger Wharf, there are now plenty of choices for a good night out. My aforementioned Australian friend introduced me to her version of the Aussie classic—the Bondi Crush. The secret is the addition of ginger and watermelon sorbet.

ON THE HI-FI
Paul Taylor and Don Spencer, *Cooee: Songs & Stories from Down Under*

Nukubati Island, Fiji

BEACHCOMBER
SERVES 4

8 oz./237ml vodka
4 oz./118ml banana
    liqueur
4 oz./118ml pear nectar
½ oz./15ml lemon juice
Fresh ginger, peeled and
thinly sliced, for garnish

In a cocktail shaker or
pitcher, mix all of the
ingredients. Pour into
glasses filled with crushed
ice, garnish with ginger
and serve.

SERVE WITH:
Brunch omelettes; sushi
and sashimi

This South Pacific paradise is a private
island in the 300-plus island archipelago
of Fiji, roughly to the east of Australia.
Nukubati's one supremely luxurious
resort caters to ardent beachgoers and
discerning gourmands. Fresh ingredients
are *de rigueur* here, whether you're
partaking in a sumptuous meal or a
luscious cocktail. The Beachcomber
combines the fruity and tart flavors of
Fiji. You can't go wrong with this drink,
especially at an impromptu outdoor
party.

nukubati island

ON THE HI-FI
Fiji Ensembles, *Music of the Fiji
Islands*

North America

From Market Street to Bourbon Street, cocktails here are a melting pot of cultures, places and people.

Los Angeles, California

THE STARLET

SERVES 4

8 oz./237ml gin
8 oz./237ml ruby-red
 grapefruit juice
2 oz./59ml lemon juice
Lemon seltzer to top
2 cups ice cubes
Fresh lemon slices and red
grapefruit slices to garnish

In a large cocktail shaker, mix gin and juices with 1 cup ice cubes. Strain mixture into ice-filled cocktail glasses. Garnish with lemon or red grapefruit slices. Serve immediately.

SERVE WITH:
Soy nuts or veggie chips

Note: For where to find star-shaped ice-cube molds, see the Resources section on page 144.

Arguably the epicenter of chic, L.A. is known for cool hotel bars like the Bar Marmont in the Chateau Marmont, or the SkyBar, perched high in West Hollywood's ultra-chic Mondrian. SkyBar is the place where stylin' Angelinos go to see and be seen while indulging in a few cocktails. The Starlet, with its citrus undertones, is a like sipping on a bit of California sunshine. It's ideal for a poolside or patio gathering, as it's delightful in batches.

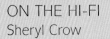

los angeles

ON THE HI-FI
Sheryl Crow

93

Santa Monica, California

IVY GIMLET

SERVES 4

- 8 oz./237ml Svedka vodka
- 2 fresh limes, plus slices for garnish
- 1 cup fresh mint leaves, plus extra for garnish

Pour vodka into a cocktail shaker. Wash and dry mint leaves, place in shaker and muddle together with the vodka for about 3 minutes. Squeeze the juice from 2 limes into the shaker, mix and let the flavors marry for a few minutes. Using a strainer, pour the mixture into ice-filled glasses. Garnish each with fresh mint and a slice of lime. Serve immediately.

SERVE WITH:

Salted cashews and almonds

Santa Monica boasts stellar shopping like Fred Segel's and Indigo Seas. When you're not strollin' on the pier, try out some of the fabulous and cool restaurants, in particular the Ivy at the Shore. Right across from the ocean and close to the pier, the location is supreme—you just might bump elbows with a Hollywood legend or two while sitting at the bar. The specialty of the house is the Ivy Gimlet, and the mint comes straight from the owner's garden. The recipe is a closely guarded secret, but here's a close approximation of it. The heavenly minty aftertaste lasts long after the drink is finished.

ON THE HI-FI
The soundtrack from *Thicker Than Water*

Rivera Maya, Mexico

MAMBO MAYA

- 8 oz./237ml premium silver tequila
- 8 oz./237ml pineapple juice
- 6 oz./177ml papaya nectar
- 4 oz./118ml coconut nectar
- 2 oz./59ml fresh lime juice

Limes and coconut spirals for garnish

Combine all ingredients in a cocktail shaker and mix well. Pour into ice-filled glasses. Slice limes and make spirals from a wedge of fresh coconut, garnish and serve immediately.

SERVE WITH:
Warm black bean dip and plantain chips

Oh, to be south of the border. Along the Caribbean coast of Mexico is a small wooden house of many colors. Here you'll find Jose, head barman and mixologist to all who find their way to him. Jose's Mambo Maya takes advantage of the area's local citrus and pineapple groves and brings all this exploding flavor together with a bit of tequila from Jose's brother's distillery. The juice makes the cocktail, so try to find the needed ingredients in specialty grocery stores or markets—it's well worth it!

ON THE HI-FI
Mambo All-Stars

Aspen, Colorado

CHOCOLATE MARTINI

SERVES 4

8 oz./237ml Absolut
  Vanilia vodka
4 oz./118ml Kahlúa
Chocolate shavings for
garnish
4 tbsp./57g raw sugar

Pour vodka and Kahlúa
into a cocktail shaker, fill
with ice, and mix well. Wet
rims of the glasses and dip
in sugar; strain mixture
into glasses. Garnish with
chocolate shavings.

SERVE WITH:
Warm spinach dip with
pita crisps and mixed nuts

Not just for snow bunnies, Aspen
attracts a glamorous ski community
that flaunts an international zip code.
This martini is named after the one
served at a longstanding institution,
the old Aspen Club Lodge, now the
very posh Sky Hotel. It's a must for
après-ski. After all, if you're out on the
slopes all day, you should reward yourself with a sweet, creamy treat.

aspen

ON THE HI-FI
Gnarls Barkley

Nashville, Tennessee

WHISKEY SMASH

SERVES 4

- 8 oz./237ml Jim Beam bourbon
- 4 mint leaves
- Half a lemon, quartered
- 1 oz./30ml simple syrup (see recipe on page 144)
- Sprig of mint

Combine all ingredients except bourbon in a large glass. Using a wooden spoon, smash the ingredients together. Add whiskey and transfer to a cocktail shaker. Shake vigorously, strain into glasses filled with crushed ice and garnish each with a sprig of mint.

SERVE WITH:
Hush puppies

Nashville is home to country music, great Southern food and whiskey. The Whiskey Smash, a classic Nashville cocktail, is a flavorful blend of bourbon, mint and lemon. It's a perfect drink to sip on a warm afternoon or serve to friends before dinner—for just the right touch of Southern hospitality.

ON THE HI-FI
Kenny Chesney

Chicago, Illinois

RHUBARB CHAMPAGNE COCKTAIL

SERVES 4

4 oz./118ml rhubarb mix
(see recipe on page 144)
4 oz./118ml Cointreau
Champagne to top
(1 bottle/750ml)
Strawberries for garnish

Pour 1 oz. of the rhubarb mix into each glass, add a splash of Cointreau and top with champagne. Garnish with a strawberry.

SERVE WITH:
Roquefort pinwheels

Nicknamed the Windy City, Chicago is home to legendary jazz, fantastic shopping, the impressive Sears Tower and great energy. The place of the moment is The Drawing Room, where they mix your cocktail tableside, how posh! The social scene is always buzzing with friends and workmates meeting up for cocktails and conversation. If the weather is too brisk outside, invite everyone in for a few of these favorites. The mix is easy to prepare and well worth the effort—any extra can be frozen for future parties.

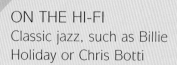

ON THE HI-FI
Classic jazz, such as Billie Holiday or Chris Botti

chicago

New York, New York

BIG APPLE MARTINI

SERVES 4

- 6 oz./177ml vodka
- 4 oz./118ml apple schnapps
- 4 oz./118ml apple purée or juice
- 2 oz./59ml lime juice

Pinch of ground cinnamon or nutmeg

Pour all of the ingredients into a cocktail shaker and add ice to fill. Shake well and strain into chilled martini glasses. Garnish with small apple slices. *HINT:* To keep the apple slices from browning on the glasses, toss them in a little lemon juice first.

SERVE WITH:
Spicy bagel chips

Known as the Big Apple, New York is truly the city that never sleeps. At the moment, rooftop bars are the ultra-chic place to be. And there is nothing better than sipping a martini while looking at the Chrysler Building and that twinkling skyline. This recipe is derived from the creations of a few favorite night spots. Apple schnapps makes the color and flavor sublime, while the spice adds just the right amount of zip.

new york

ON THE HI-FI
Frank Sinatra

BAREFOOT BLISS MARGARITA

SERVES 4

- 8 oz./237ml blanco tequila
- 4 oz./118ml Cointreau
- 2 oz./59ml lime juice
- 2 oz./59ml lemon juice
- 4 cups/950ml crushed ice

Coarse salt for glass rims (optional)

2 limes, thinly sliced, for garnish

Combine the first four ingredients in a large shaker or pitcher, fill with ice and mix well. Salt the rims of glasses, pour drinks and garnish with fresh lime slices.

SERVE WITH:
Shrimp and a citrus-infused cocktail sauce

Can't hop in the copter and head out to the east end of Long Island for the weekend? Don't worry—here's a recipe for the cocktail favored by most of the Hamptonites (East-Enders) and the jet-setting vacation crowd. Have more than one and you'll be virtually walking barefoot on the beach. This classic margarita is filled with robust flavor; the addition of lemon juice completes its clean, crisp citrus tones.

east hampton

ON THE HI-FI
Anything by Jimmy Buffett

Nantucket, Massachusetts

ISLAND GIRL
SERVES 4

8 oz./237ml cranberry
juice
8 oz./237ml vodka
4 oz./118ml ginger ale
2 oz./59ml lime juice
Lime slices for garnish

Mix all ingredients in a
large pitcher. Pour into ice-
filled glasses and serve.
Garnish with lime slices.

SERVE WITH:
Seared scallops drizzled
with vinaigrette; clams on
the half-shell with a good
cocktail sauce; for landlubbers, try ½ cup cranberry
chutney over an 8-oz.
block of cream cheese and
serve with crackers

An island off the coast of Cape Cod,
Nantucket was once the whaling
capital of the world. Now it's a classy
summertime vacation spot for Boston
and New York's well-to-do. From the
scent of wild roses to the smell of the
sea, heady fragrances fill the air. With
plenty of pristine public beaches, tony
inns and boutiques, there is much to
do here. Nantucket also boasts large
cranberry bogs, so it's appropriate that
the island's signature cocktail uses this
pungent juice. The RopeWalk restaurant
right on Straight Wharf makes this
exceptionally good concoction. Put on
some preppy togs and get mixing!

ON THE HI-FI
Chris Isaak, *Baja Sessions*

nantucket

Miami, Florida

BAY BREEZE
SERVES 4

8 oz./237ml vodka
4 oz./118ml orange juice
4 oz./118ml pineapple
   juice
4 oz./118ml mango juice
Splash of lime juice
1 lime for garnish

Pour all ingredients into a shaker, add ice and mix well. Strain into ice-filled glasses. Garnish with lime wedges.

SERVE WITH:
Fried plantains with black-bean dip; a big platter of jumbo shrimp with a tropi-cal-flavored sauce

In Miami, you'll find magnificent houses lining boat-filled waterways, sun-drenched beaches and a bevy of people working hard for that lovely bronze glow. But if you want action, it all happens after the sun goes down—when the lights come on, the strip gets hot and cocktail hour in Miami gets underway. This libation was a regular feature on Miami Vice in the '80s, and it remains a local favorite. The traditional Bay Breeze cocktail has a bit more fruit juice, but this version eliminates some of that excess sweetness.

miami

ON THE HI-FI
Ricky Martin or Enrique Iglesias

Key Largo, Florida

RUM RUNNER
SERVES 4

6 oz./177ml Bacardi dark rum
2 oz./59ml blackberry brandy
2 oz./59ml banana liqueur
Splash of grenadine
Splash of lime juice
Meyer's rum for floaters

Mix all ingredients in a blender filled with ice. Blend until smooth. Pour into glasses, garnish with straws and slices of fresh lime. Top with rum floater if desired.

SERVE WITH:
Fried clams with dipping sauce; or, for landlubbers, a bowl of salted mixed nuts

Down Key Largo way, there is a place that has the most incredible sunsets: the Ocean Reef Club. After a day of swimming, lounging in the sun and snorkeling off the reefs, nothing tastes better than a frozen Rum Runner. This refreshing cooler is perfect for any warm weather gathering. Although it's powerful on its own, it really takes off if you top it with a floater of Meyer's rum—just like they serve it down on the reef.

ON THE HI-FI
Steel drums or reggae

key largo

South America

Everything flows to Latin rhythms and the energy is as electrifying as the social scene; the cocktails are no exception.

Santiago, Chile

PISCO SOUR

12 oz./355ml Pisco ABA
 4 tsp./20ml key-lime
   juice
 6 tsp./30ml simple syrup
   see recipe on page 144)
 2 egg whites

Mix all ingredients in a
cocktail shaker filled with
ice, shake well and strain
into ice-filled glasses.
Serve immediately.

SERVE WITH:
Fresh oysters on the half-
shell; cocktail shrimp
sprinkled with lemon; a
sharp semisoft cheese with
grapes and crackers

Surrounded by the snowy peaks of the
Andes, Chile's capital, founded in the
16th century by a Spanish conquistador,
is home to beautiful parks, museums
and an abundance of universities, and
will soon be home to the tallest building in South America. In this
thriving, modern metropolis, you will
find the tastiest Pisco Sours ever
made. Most bartenders here use key
limes instead of lemons. The bite of
the limes adds a unique spin to the
very fine Pisco ABA, a Chilean variety
of brandy made from white muscat
grapes and possessing a floral essence.
The PS is a classic cocktail, just perfect
for mixing up a batch for friends
anytime.

ON THE HI-FI
Soft music with Latin influences,
such as Buena Vista Social Club
or Gipsy Kings

Rio de Janeiro, Brazil

SEXY BACK
SERVES 4

8 oz./237ml premium
   silver tequila
8 oz./237ml lychee juice
8 oz./237ml Cointreau
Splash of lime juice
Edible flowers for garnish
(one for each glass)

In an ice-filled cocktail
shaker, combine all
ingredients and mix well.
Pour into chilled glasses,
garnish each with a
flower and serve.

SERVE WITH:
A variety of salted
Brazilian nuts

Rio, known as "the Marvelous City,"
beckons with its splendid beaches, the
throbbing pulse of samba and the
magical backdrop of the famed Sugar
Loaf Mountain. The famed Copacabana
Palace, a neoclassical gem dating from
the 1920s, has been home to the likes
of Edith Piaf, national legend Carmen
Miranda and Orson Welles. At the
Copa, as the locals call it, they serve a
delicious drink that's colorful and
always shaken, not stirred. Here's our
sublime SB.

ON THE HI-FI
Celso Fonseca, *Natural*

Sao Paulo, Brazil

CAIPIRINHA

SERVES 4

- 8 oz./237ml cachaça
- 2 limes, cut into eighths
- ¼ cup/57g natural brown sugar

Muddle 4 lime wedges and 2 tsp. sugar in each glass. Fill glasses with crushed ice. Pour 2 oz. cachaça into each glass and stir. Top with crushed ice.

SERVE WITH:

Roasted figs stuffed with goat cheese

One of the largest metropolitan regions in the world, Sao Paolo is equally big on style. Filled with sleekly designed hotels, great international cuisine and tons of culture, it's dubbed South America's New York City. Located in the chic Jardins neighborhood, Hotel Emiliano boasts a minimalist bar where wonderful drinks are served. To follow suit and add a little heat to your gatherings, transport your mind, body and spirit to a carnival state with a Caipirinha, the country's national drink. Made with cachaça, a Brazilian liquor distilled directly from sugarcane, this libation packs quite the punch.

ON THE HI-FI
Elis Regina, *Essential Elis Vol. 1*

Buenos Aires, Argentina

SLINGSHOT
SERVES 4

- 8 oz./237ml dark rum
- 6 oz./177ml apricot brandy
- 8 oz./237ml orange juice
- 4 oz./118ml pineapple juice

Dash of grenadine
Rum floater if desired
Cherries and pineapple wedges for garnish

Combine all ingredients in a cocktail pitcher and mix well. Pour into glasses filled with crushed ice. Float additional rum if desired. Garnish each glass with cherries and a pineapple wedge. Serve immediately.

SERVE WITH:
Empanadas with dipping sauces

The territory of tango dancing, strong coffee and all things hip and happening, the city of BA is hotter than ever. Here, 2 A.M. means the night is still young. A great cocktail to sip while taking it all in is the Slingshot. This potent beverage has a "dark side" in its rum, while the citrus juices give it bursts of light. Perfect for a night with friends and throwing a few steaks on the grill.

ON THE HI-FI
Los Fabulosos Cadillacs or Bajofondo Tango Club

Caribbean

Create your own party paradise
with these fruit-filled libations
direct from nature's bounty.

Havana, Cuba

THE PAPA DOBLE
SERVES 4

- 8 oz./237ml light rum
- 4 oz./118ml maraschino liqueur
- 8 oz./237ml fresh grapefruit juice
- 2 oz./59ml fresh lime juice

Fresh grapefruit for garnish

Put all ingredients in blender with 2 cups of ice cubes and blend well. Pour into glasses and garnish with grapefruit wedges. If desired, sweeten to taste with a bit of sugar.

SERVE WITH:
Black-bean quesadillas

Once home to Ernest Hemingway, the gracious capital city of Cuba has a rich history. As the renovation of hotels and restaurants is on the rise, there is a resurgence of architecture, art and a booming social scene in Old Havana. The Papa Doble is a daiquiri version named after Hemingway, who, after hitting his writing for a few hours, would venture out to quench his thirst and socialize. The tang of the grapefruit juice in this drink does wonders on a hot day. Put down the novel, make a batch and drink up!

havana

ON THE HI-FI
Afro-Cuban All-Stars

Paradise Island, Bahamas

PIÑA COLADA

SERVES 4

- 8 oz./237ml light rum
- 8 oz./237ml pineapple juice
- 4 oz./118ml Coco Lopez Cream of Coconut
- 2 oz./59ml fresh lime juice

Fresh pineapple wedges and coconut shavings for garnish

Mix all ingredients together, add 2 cups of ice and blend on high speed. Pour into glasses and garnish with pineapple wedges and coconut shavings. Serve immediately.

SERVE WITH:
Conch fritters

Ahh…the famed One&Only Ocean Club, where, after a multimillion-dollar renovation, part of the 2006 James Bond movie *Casino Royale* was filmed. All you need to do to get a drink here is hold up a flag (provided especially for this reason) and a waiter will come along to take your order. The specialty of the house, the Piña Colada, is absolutely delicious—it must be the addition of refreshingly zesty lime juice.

ON THE HI-FI
Barrington "Fat Cat" Hawkins, *Feel It in the Music*

Round Hill, Jamaica

RUM AROUND

SERVES 4

- 10 oz./296ml pineapple juice
- 4 oz./118ml light rum
- 4 oz./118ml dark rum
- 2 oz./59ml coconut nectar
- 2 oz./59ml cherry juice

Fresh pineapple slices and maraschino cherries for garnish

Mix ingredients together in a pitcher and pour into ice-filled glasses. Garnish with pineapple slices and cherries.

SERVE WITH:
Plantain chips and fruit-based salsa; order-in BBQ

Is Bob Marley's sunny island calling you? Are you in need of a tropical retreat without too much effort? Jamaica, with its balmy breezes and pineapple trees, is filled with historic plantation houses that have been turned into first-class hotels such as the Pineapple House (designed by Ralph Lauren) in Montego Bay's Round Hill resort. Just steps from the sandy beach, you can treat yourself to the Rum Around, the infamous cocktail mixed by head barman Kingsley. Garnished with cherries and a wedge of fresh pineapple, this sweet, cheering libation will have you and your guests partying island-style in no time!

round hill

ON THE HI-FI
Bob Marley, Harry Belafonte or the Mambo Kings

131

Turks and Caicos

TEQUILA SUNRISE
SERVES 4

8 oz./237ml white tequila

12 oz./355ml orange juice

2 oz./59ml fresh lime juice

2 oz./59ml grenadine

Orange slices and cherries for garnish

Fill glasses with ice. In a shaker, mix tequila, orange juice and lime juice. Pour evenly into glasses. Slowly pour the grenadine into each glass, forming a swirl effect. Add an orange slice and a cherry as garnish and serve immediately.

SERVE WITH:
Potato skins stuffed with goat-cheese spread

Just an hour's flight from Miami, this tiny private spa island casts a spell of tranquility and recuperation from life's cares. The cocktail to ask for after you've had your afternoon swim should be the Tequila Sunrise. It's surprisingly fresh, and the touch of lime adds a tangy zest. The "sunrise" part of the drink's name comes from the effect of the grenadine slowly spreading through the juices—so beautiful, and like the sun, it will warm you through and through.

ON THE HI-FI
Glen Medeiros, *Captured*

Cat Cay, Bahamas

CAT CAY PUNCH
SERVES 4

8 oz./237ml dark rum
4 oz./118ml light rum
8 oz./237ml pineapple juice
8 oz./237ml passionfruit nectar
2 oz./59ml fresh lime juice
Lime wedges for garnish

Combine all the ingredients into a cocktail shaker and mix well. Pour into ice-filled glasses. Garnish with lime wedges and serve.

SERVE WITH:
Conch salad and potato crisps

Cat Cay is a small, privately owned island in the Bimini chain of islands that form part of the Bahamas. It is a quiet respite, a palm-tree paradise with pristine white sand beaches and a coveted languor. The island is known for the specialty cocktail that is served at the wonderfully scenic bar at the end of the dock. Bu's Bar keeps a tight rein on the ingredients of this secret recipe, but the one here is a very close facsimile. It's a perfect drink in either summer or midwinter.

ON THE HI-FI
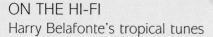
Harry Belafonte's tropical tunes

St. Barts, West Indies

FIREFLY

SERVES 4

- 8 oz./237ml light rum
- 8 oz./237ml mango purée
- 8 oz./237ml orange juice
- 6 oz./177ml apricot liqueur
- 1 oz./30ml lemon juice
- 1 oz./30ml lime juice
- 4 cups/950ml crushed ice

Fresh mango wedges for garnish

Pour ingredients into blender and add the ice. Blend until smooth, adding more ice if necessary. Pour mixture into glasses and garnish with a wedge of fresh mango.

SERVE WITH:
Pineapple pizzas

If you can't jet down to this Caribbean destination for the weekend or weren't invited aboard a mega-yacht to ring in the new year, don't worry—you can still indulge in the island's most popular cocktail. This is a slightly less sweet version than the Fireflies they mix up on Shell Beach, where touristas flock to pick up shells, catch the sun and be part of the scene.

ON THE HI-FI
Bob Marley or any steel drum favorites

Marigot, St. Martin

LA VIE EN ROSE
SERVES 4

- 1 cup sliced fresh strawberries
- 2 oz./59ml simple syrup (see recipe on page 144)
- 1 oz./30ml fresh lime juice
- 4 oz./118ml Absolut Kurant vodka
- 1 bottle (750 ml) dry champagne

A few strawberry slices for garnish

You can't go wrong on a Caribbean isle with both a French and a Dutch side—there's something for everyone here. Sunset cocktails are especially enticing at La Vie en Rose, a wonderful restaurant overlooking the harbor of Marigot, the capital of the French side. It's *très romantique*! This cocktail is named after this famous eatery. I suggest chilling the champagne glasses and using only fresh strawberries, as frozen berries contain too much syrup. Raspberries or blackberries also go nicely with the dry champagne.

Mix the strawberries, syrup and lime together in a shaker, add the vodka and fill with ice. Shake and strain evenly into chilled champagne flutes. Top with champagne and garnish with a sliced strawberry.

SERVE WITH:
Goat-cheese dumplings

ON THE HI-FI
Isabelle Boulay

Mustique, West Indies

MUDSLIDE
SERVES 4

- 6 oz./177ml Kahlúa
- 6 oz./177ml Absolut Vanilia vodka
- 4 oz./118ml Baileys Irish Cream

Whipped cream for floating

Pour all ingredients into blender and add 2 cups of ice cubes. Blend until smooth. Pour mixture into glasses and top each with a whipped cream floater. You may also top with a Kahlúa floater if desired. Serve immediately.

SERVE WITH:
Sweet potato chips

This tinyish, isolated private island is packed with glam power—celebs aplenty bunk up here—but the biggest star on the island has to be Basil's Bar. Located right on the beach, it serves up some unforgettable cocktails, one of the most popular being the Mudslide. This is the closest I could come to the recipe—if you ask at the bar, you'll get a little of this, a little of that, and not the entire truth. But my version of the frozen drink is extremely popular with friends all over the world—I have e-mail photos of their famous house parties to prove it. Go ahead whip up a batch or two and let your party begin.

ON THE HI-FI
Bruddah Kruz, *Talkin' da Kine*

Bermuda

RUM SWIZZLE
SERVES 4

8 oz./237ml dark rum
8 oz./237ml soda water
2 oz./59ml fresh lime
  juice
4 tsp./19g raw sugar
4 dashes of bitters
Fresh lime wedges for
garnish

In pitcher, mix lime juice,
sugar and soda water and
divide mixture equally
among glasses. Fill glasses
with ice, then add the rum
and bitters. Garnish with
fresh lime wedges and
serve with swizzle sticks.

SERVE WITH:
Huntsman cheese with
crackers and stuffed olives

Land of Bermuda shorts and pink-sand
beaches, this island is home to some
famous faces. Hotels are plentiful and
the ocean is a wonderful temperature.
The signature drinks you'll find are the
Rum Swizzle (as popularized by the
Swizzle Inn in Baileys Bay) and the
Dark and Stormy. I prefer the Swizzle,
as it puts me in mind of kicking back
and watching an afternoon cricket
match with friends. The swizzle refers
to a stick used to stir and dissolve the
sugar, which helps gently sweeten the
drink—any good stirrer will do.

bermuda

ON THE HI-FI
Peter Allen, *The Very Best Of*

143

Recipes

* SIMPLE SYRUP

Simple syrup is a key ingredient in many cocktail recipes, as a sweetener that incorporates easily into most drinks.

To make simple syrup:

MAKES SCANT 1 CUP

Combine 1 cup water and 1 cup sugar in a saucepan and bring to a boil. Stir constantly until the sugar has dissolved and the liquid is clear, about 5 minutes. Remove from the heat and let cool. The syrup will keep, refrigerated in a sealed jar or container, for up to one week.

* LEMON GRASS INFUSION:
(for Lemon Grass Crush, Hong Kong, China)

12 inches/30.5cm lemon grass
 1 tsp./5g sugar
 8 oz./237ml water

In small saucepan, place lemon grass and water and bring to a boil. Continue boiling until mixture is reduced by one half; add sugar and strain. Cool.

* RHUBARB MIX
(for Rhubarb Champagne Cocktail, Chicago, IL)

 2 stalks rhubarb
 1 cup strawberries, washed, with tops removed
 1 tsp./5g vanilla extract
 1 tsp./5g sugar

Juice of 1 fresh lime

Purée all ingredients except lime. Reduce liquid to one-half its volume over heat. Add lime juice. The mix can be stored in an air-tight container in the refrigerator for up to one week.

Resources

CRATE&BARREL
crate&barrel.com

HOMEGOODS
www.homegoods.com

WILLIAMS-SONOMA
www.williams-sonoma.com

Bar Lingo

Dash
A very small amount usually splashed into the drink.

Float/Floater
A topper for a cocktail or drink. The floater can be, for instance, rum, meaning a small pour on top of the drink, or a floater of whipped cream on top of a coffee cocktail.

Muddle
Crushing fruit and/or herbs in the bottom of a tall glass with a wooden pestle or "muddler" to release their juices and flavors in a concentrated fashion.

Strain
After a drink has been mixed, straining is often required to discard any bits of fruit or seeds, etc. Most cocktail shakers come with a strainer. If yours does not, any mesh strainer will do.

Shaking
Place all of the ingredients in the shaker and fill with ice to just below the rim. Put the top on tightly and shake with sass and style. About twenty seconds is good—if you overshake, you will dilute the cocktail.

Swizzle stick
Fancy name for a stirrer, the swizzle stick is sometimes made from sugar or honey; it has a dual purpose: adding sweetness to the drink as it dissolves, while mixing bits of herbs or fruit that may have settled to the bottom of the glass.

Garnish
Any decorative element added to a cocktail, such as fruit, olives, herbs, coffee beans, flowers, or chocolate shavings. Often it is a combination of two or more.

Bar Basics

GLASSWARE

Champagne flute   Highball   Martini   Rocks   Sling   Hurricane   Irish coffee   Coupette

GARNISHES:
* lemons
* limes
* olives
* cocktail onions
* maraschino cherries
* mint leaves
* coarse salt
* Turbinado (raw sugar)
* fresh fruit, such as pineapple, strawberries, kiwi, oranges, etc.
* chocolate shavings
* coconut shavings
* cucumber slices
* lychee fruit
* cranberries

MISCELLANEOUS:
* cocktail shaker with strainer
* ice cube trays
* stirrers
* straws
* picks
* coasters
* napkins
* small dishes for snacks
* blender for frozen drinks

Index

147